MAGICAL CITIES

by John Hamilton

Published by ABDO Publishing Company, 4940 Viking Drive, Suite 622, Edina, Minnesota 55435.
Copyright ©2006 by Abdo Consulting Group, Inc. International copyrights reserved in all countries.
No part of this book may be reproduced in any form without written permission from the publisher.
ABDO & Daughters™ is a trademark and logo of ABDO Publishing Company.

Printed in the United States.

Editor: Paul Joseph
Graphic Design: John Hamilton
Cover Design: TDI
Cover Illustration: *Soldiers of Paradise* ©1987 Don Maitz
Interior Photos and Illustrations: p 1 *Soldiers of Paradise* ©1987 Don Maitz; p 4 King Arthur tapestry, Corbis; p 5 Alcazar Castle, Corbis; p 6 scene from *King Arthur*, Corbis; p 7 Arthur Rackham painting of King Arthur, Mary Evans Picture Library; p 8 page from de Troyes, Corbis; p 9 *The Death of Arthur*, Corbis; p 10 Cadbury hilltop, Corbis; p 11 Tintagel Castle, Corbis; p 12-13 *Arthur Knights Lancelot* ©1996 Don Maitz; p 14 Atlantic Hotel aquarium, Corbis; p 16 (top) satellite view of Santorini, NOAA; p 16 (bottom) map of Atlantis, Corbis; p 17 (top) deep-sea diver, Mary Evan Picture Library; p 17 (bottom) Captain Nemo, Wikipedia; p 18 Valkyrie, Corbis; p 19 Odin, Corbis; p 20 scene from *The Road to El Dorado*, courtesy Dreamworks SKG; p 21 Sir Walter Raleigh, Corbis; p 22 portrait of J.R.R. Tolkien, Corbis; p 23 (top) Gandalf arrives at Minas Tirith, courtesy New Line Cinema; p 23 (bottom) *The Return of the King* book cover, courtesy Houghton Mifflin; p 24 (top) Minas Tirith, courtesy New Line Cinema; p 25 (bottom) cavalry charge at Pelennor Fields, courtesy New Line Cinema; p 25 (top) Aragorn leads his army, courtesy New Line Cinema; p 25 (bottom) fell beast, courtesy New Line Cinema; p 26 Frodo at Rivendell, courtesy New Line Cinema; p 27 Rivendell, courtesy New Line Cinema; p 28 Marco Polo meets Kublai Kahn, Corbis; p 29 (top) *The Forbidden City*, Corbis; p 29 (bottom) Kublai Kahn, Corbis.

Library of Congress Cataloging-in-Publication Data

Hamilton, John, 1959–
    Magical Cities / John Hamilton
       p. cm. — (Fantasy & folklore)
    Includes index.
    ISBN 1-59679-338-4
    1. Geographical myths. 2. Cities and towns. 3. Folklore. I. Title

GR940.H36 2005
398'.42—dc22

                                              2005048314

CONTENTS

Camelot

amelot was the most important castle-city in all the legends of King Arthur and his Knights of the Round Table. It was the place where Arthur ruled over medieval Britain. With its thick castle walls and brilliant white towers, Camelot shone like a beacon of light over a land filled with darkness and peril. It was here that Arthur created a utopia governed by chivalry, justice, and order, and where "fight only for the good" was every knight's motto.

But was Camelot a real place? The oldest stories of King Arthur don't mention Camelot by name. In fact, we're not even sure of Arthur's identity, and without Arthur there can be no Camelot.

There are many opinions of who exactly this warrior-king really was. Most scholars believe Arthur is a character made up from many legends and folktales. In real-life, he may have been Artorius, a Britain of Celt ancestry who was trained by the Roman military. Artorius was a skilled cavalry commander, first mentioned in a Welsh poem written by Gododdin around 600 A.D., many years after the great king's death.

Left: King Arthur, a detail from a 14th-century Flemish tapestry.
Facing page: A full moon rises over Alcazar Castle in Segovia, a far-away echo of what Camelot once was.

The Roman Empire held Britain as a province for more than 400 years. But by 407 A.D., the Romans began pulling back their armies. The Empire was crumbling, and it needed all of its military forces to protect Rome from foreign invaders. When the Romans finally abandoned Britain altogether, the land fell into a loose collection of Celtic-style tribes who sometimes squabbled and fought among themselves.

By the late 5th century, Britain was wide open to conquest by barbarian hordes. The only thing stopping the invaders, especially the fearsome Saxons, were the groups of brave warriors left behind by the Romans.

Luckily, Artorius was a military genius who led the native Britons to 12 great victories against armies of the Saxons, Picts, Scots, and Irish. When Arthur drew his sword, according to one Welsh legend, "flames of fire might be seen as from the mouths of serpents, and so dreadful was he that none could look upon him."

At the dawn of the 6th century, Artorius led his armored knights against the Saxon shield wall at the Battle of Badon Hill. The barbarian infantry was shattered, and the survivors fled in terror. More than 900 Saxons lay dead upon the field of battle. The victory was so complete that the Saxons were forced to ask for peace. For three decades, few barbarian armies dared challenge the might of the British and their brilliant leader, Artorius.

Right: Arthur rides with his knights in this scene from the movie *King Arthur.*
Facing page: King Arthur uses his sword Excalibur in this painting by Arthur Rackham.

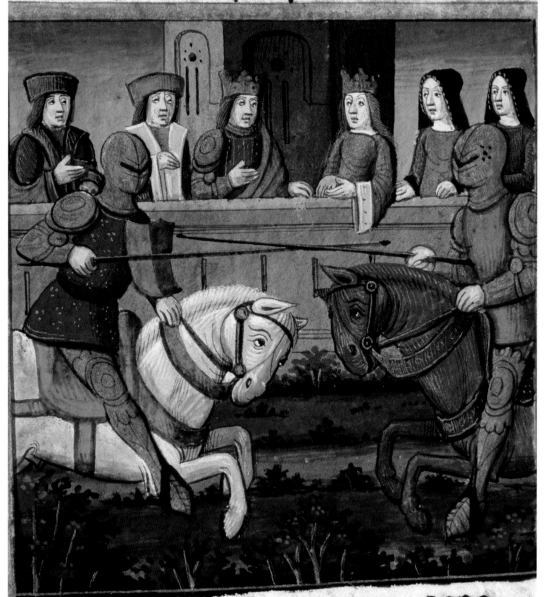

uant ilz furēt tous aſſēblez e
prez de lzaamalot Galaad pa
la priere du roy et de la royne miſt ſo

Artorius's victories brought relative peace to the land, and glory to Britain. Even though the Saxons would later conquer Britain, Artorius bought precious time for the native Celts to preserve parts of their way of life. His deeds, and those of his knights, were passed down, generation to generation, through songs and folktales. Over the centuries, the stories were written down and then changed, little by little, until the King Arthur we know today became Britain's national hero.

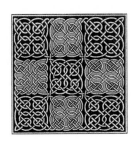

Poets and writers added many parts of the Arthur legends that we know in this day and age. Writers such as Geoffrey of Monmouth, Sir Thomas Mallory, and even Mark Twain, have all added parts to the puzzle that is King Arthur. Tales of the sword in the stone, the quest for the Holy Grail, and Excalibur, are the stuff of legend and folklore, not to be found in history books.

Is Camelot also just a legend? Was it invented by storytellers to give Arthur and his knights a convenient home base? Many historians think so. They suggest that Camelot isn't a real place at all. Instead, they say, Camelot is an *idea* that represents all that is good about Arthur and his followers—helping those in need, justice for all, might for right. They point out that Camelot isn't even mentioned by name in the Arthur legends until the 12th century. French author Chrétien de Troyes wrote *Lancelot* many hundreds of years after Arthur would have lived.

Left: The Death of Arthur, by John Mulcaster Carrick. *Facing page:* A page from Crétien de Troyes's book *Romance of King Arthur,* showing a jousting match in front of King Arthur and Queen Guenevere.

Facing page: The ruins of Tintagel Castle. It is one possible location of Camelot. It is also the rumored place where King Arthur was born.
Below: The hilltop near Cadbury, in southwestern England, where some believe Camelot may have once stood.

Different authors have placed the legendary Camelot in many areas all over Britain. In *Le Morte d'Arthur*, 15th century author Sir Thomas Malory wrote that Camelot was in Winchester, in southern England. In 1136, Geoffrey of Monmouth, in his *History of the Kings of Britain*, said Camelot was actually Caerleon Castle in Wales. Tintagel, a fortress in Cornwall (and also Arthur's supposed birthplace) is yet another possible location. Most serious scholars doubt that any of these places were actually used by the historical King Arthur.

John Leland, a 14th century author, claimed that Camelot once existed near the site of Cadbury Castle, in Somerset, southwestern England. Local tradition said that a nearby hill was called "Camalat." The hill rises 250 feet (76 m) above the surrounding land, a perfect place for a fort or castle.

Archeologists in the 1960s traveled to the hill and began excavating. To their surprise, they unearthed the remains of a ruined fortress. There were many large buildings, which meant that it could have been a center of trade, or a military stronghold. By examining the stone walls, plus coins and pottery found on the site, the archeologists decided that the Celt fortress was probably built around 450 to 500 A.D. It's very possible that Artorius, the historical King Arthur, could have used the castle as his home base.

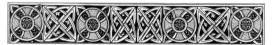

No direct evidence, no real proof, has been found linking Arthur to Cadbury Castle. But there are other tantalizing clues. A nearby river is called River Cam. Legend says that Arthur fought his last battle, and received a fatal wound, at the Battle of Camlann.

The abbey at Glastonbury Tor is 12 miles (19 km) to the north. It was there, in the year 1190, that monks claimed they had discovered the bones of Arthur and his queen, Guinevere. A lead cross was also found, with the inscription, "Here lies the famous King Arthur, buried in the isle of Avalon."

The cross and the bones were later lost during centuries of strife and warfare. But local tradition says King Arthur wasn't buried in the abbey anyway. The folktales say that the great king was buried in a hidden cave at Cadbury, near his beloved city fortress of Camelot. And twice a year, on Midsummer Eve and Christmas Eve, legend says, "you can hear Arthur rising from his tomb and riding down from Camelot to drink from the ancient spring that bears his name."

Right: Arthur Knights Lancelot, by Don Maitz.

ATLANTIS

tlantis was a legendary island, a mysterious lost civilization that sank to the bottom of the ocean thousands of years ago, never to be found again. The people of Atlantis were an advanced race. Their government and technology were far ahead of other civilizations. Some say Atlantis was originally populated by a race of space aliens, who wisely shared their technology with emerging human civilizations.

Then, a catastrophe struck: A tremendous earthquake, or perhaps a tsunami, destroyed Atlantis, submerging the island. Some claim it wasn't a natural disaster at all, that the Atlanteans finally destroyed themselves with nuclear bombs or some other destructive technology. But after the calamity, some legends say, a handful of the inhabitants survived to rebuild their civilization. To this day, they rule a secret underwater world filled with technological marvels.

People have been searching for the real Atlantis for many years. The trouble is, it's a very old story, with puzzling clues and shifting facts.

The first written mention of Atlantis comes from Plato, the philosopher who lived in ancient Greece from 427 B.C. to about 347 B.C. He was a very wise and influential teacher.

Facing page: The Atlantis Hotel, a resort in the Bahamas, created this aquarium to resemble the fabled lost city. It holds over 50,000 fish.

Two of Plato's writings, *Timaeus* and *Critias*, discuss Atlantis. Plato said Atlantis was located somewhere in the ocean, beyond the "Pillars of Hercules," which many scholars think refers to the Strait of Gibraltar. The strait is a narrow section of water separating the Mediterranean Sea and the Atlantic Ocean. Plato said the ancient civilization was destroyed by an earthquake or tsunami. This happened 9,000 years before Plato was born. The story, he said, was passed down by ancient Egyptians.

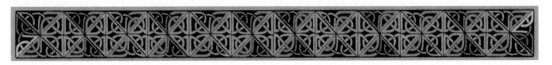

Some people today think that Atlantis sank in the mid-Atlantic Ocean. Others believe it was actually in the Mediterranean Sea. Different theories place the mythical land all over the world, from Cuba, to the Andes Mountains, even to Antarctica!

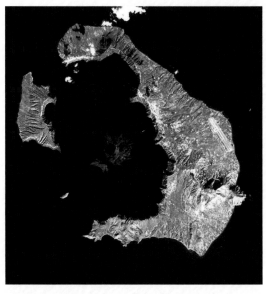

Right: A satellite view of the island of Santorini. Could Atlantis once have existed here?
Below: A 17th-century map claiming to show the location of Atlantis.

One of the most serious examinations of the legend places Atlantis at Santorini. Also known as Thera, Santorini is a small, circular group of volcanic islands in the Aegean Sea, east of Greece. Geologists know that thousands of years ago a tremendous eruption occurred, devastating the Minoan civilization that lived in the area. A volcano could have produced the earthquakes and tsunamis described by Plato.

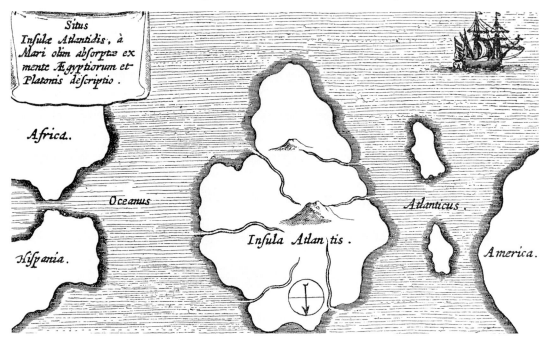

We will probably never know for sure if Atlantis really once existed, or where it was located. Most scholars believe that Plato created a piece of fiction in order to tell a story with a moral. In Plato's tale, the citizens of Atlantis became greedy, warlike, and terrorized their neighbors. The Gods became angry and caused Atlantis to be swallowed by the sea. It's a cautionary tale Plato used to teach youth about the dangers of abusing power.

Author Kevin Christopher wrote, "Atlantis continues to captivate people's imagination because it offers the hope that lost ideals or some untapped human potential will someday be uncovered."

Like King Arthur's court at Camelot, Atlantis represents things that are good about mankind. Our wish to find Atlantis mirrors our desire to rediscover simplicity and goodness in our complicated world.

Top: A deep-sea diver discovers Atlantis.
Left: Captain Nemo visits Atlantis in Jules Verne's *20,000 Leagues Under The Sea.*

Valhalla

alhalla is the home, or great hall, of Odin, the supreme god of Norse mythology. People such as the Vikings worshiped Odin. His role in their religion was complex. He represented both wisdom and war.

Odin ruled from Valhalla, which is located in Asgard, the realm of the Norse gods. Odin chose certain warriors to live with him. Norse myths said that if a warrior was gloriously slain in battle, Odin would welcome him to live at Valhalla in the afterlife. Norse goddesses called Valkyries chose the most heroic among the dead and escorted their spirits to Valhalla.

Odin's great hall had 540 doors, with walls made of spears and a roof made of shields. Benches were made of breastplates and other armor. A wolf lurked at the western door, and an eagle hovered nearby. Nobody knows exactly how big Valhalla was, but it was said that there was always room enough for those chosen to live there.

Facing page: The Norse god Odin, seated on his throne in Valhalla. *Below:* A Valkyrie rides to the battlefield.

Slain warriors at Valhalla spent their day assisting Odin, and preparing for the final battle against the wicked giants of Norse myth. This battle was called Ragnarok, the final battle between good and evil.

To prepare for the coming war, the spirits of the slain warriors marched every day to the plains of Asgard, armed for battle. There, they practiced combat among themselves. At the end of the day, those who were slain rose up again, and everyone went back inside the walls of Valhalla. At night they fed on roasted boar and drank mead.

Norse myth says that when the battle of Ragnarok finally comes, 800 warriors will march out each door of Valhalla, shoulder to shoulder, ready to help Odin in the final war at the end of the world.

EL DORADO

When Spanish conquistadors explored the New World in the 16th century, they heard tales of a fabulous city made entirely of gold, which was hidden deep in the jungles of South America. The city came to be known as El Dorado. It lured European explorers for almost two centuries, but it was never found.

Legends were told of a mythical tribe of people who ruled the northern part of South America. Each year a chief was rolled in gold dust, which completely covered his skin. (In the Spanish language, *El Dorado* means "The Gilded One.") Then, in a sacred ceremony, the chief was washed off in a nearby lake. Emeralds and gold were also tossed into the water as offerings to the gods. The city where the chief ruled was said to be fabulously wealthy. Even the streets were paved with pure gold. The Spanish dubbed the city El Dorado, but it was also known as Manoa, or Omoan.

The legends started a frenzy of exploration. Gonzalo Pizarro and Francisco de Orellana were two of the first who tried finding the fabled city of gold. Other explorers included Philipp von Hutten, Diego de Ordaz, and many others. None of the expeditions found El Dorado. Most ended in starvation, disease, or death.

In 1595, Sir Walter Raleigh, the famous English explorer, searched for El Dorado by investigating parts of the Orinoco River in Guyana, South America. He returned to England empty-handed, the expedition having accomplished very little. But he wrote an account of the expedition and claimed to have discovered the city's location on an island in Parima Lake, in Guyana. Until the claim was later disproved, El Dorado was marked on maps of South America for nearly two centuries.

Facing page: Sir Walter Raleigh, the English explorer who claimed to have discovered El Dorado.
Below: A scene from Dreamworks' animated motion picture, *The Road to El Dorado.*

MINAS TIRITH

inas Tirith is the capital of the land of Gondor in J.R.R. Tolkien's fantasy world of Middle-earth. It plays an important part in *The Lord of the Rings* series of books.

Minas Tirith serves as the last stronghold of mankind against the evil flowing from the nearby land of Mordor. The menacing

villain Sauron knows that to conquer Middle-earth, he must destroy Minas Tirith, and so unleashes his armies of orcs against the city.

The people of Gondor live in a military society with a highly developed culture, much like ancient Greece or Rome. Minas Tirith is their main fortress. It is an ancient city where the Gondorian kings live.

When the kingdom of Gondor was first settled, the capital was Osgiliath. Minas Tirith was a fortress originally known as Minas Anor, and it had a sister city called Minas Ithil (the Tower of the Moon).

The sister city was captured by the evil ringwraiths, servants of Sauron, and

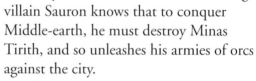

Left: J.R.R. Tolkien, author of *The Lord of the Rings.*

renamed Minas Morgul. Gondor's ancient King Tarondor moved the royal court to Minas Anor and renamed it Minas Tirith, which means, "Tower of the Guard." It is from Minas Tirith that the forces of Gondor shield Middle-earth from the shadow of Mordor.

Minas Tirith is sometimes called the White City. Its walls and buildings are carved out of marble, and it appears to glow in the sunlight. In the third book of the trilogy, *The Return of the King*, Tolkien described the hobbit Pippin seeing Minas Tirith for the first time:

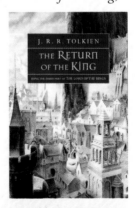

...the Guarded City, with its seven walls of stone so strong and old that it seemed to have been not builded but carven by giants out of the stones of the earth.

Even as Pippin gazed in wonder the walls passed from looming grey to white, blushing faintly in the dawn; and suddenly the sun climbed over the eastern shadow and

Above: The wizard Gandalf arrives at Minas Tirith.
Left: The cover of the book, *The Return of the King*, shows a scene from Minas Tirith.

Above: Minas Tirith shines in the sunlight, while the lands of Mordor glow ominously in the distance.

Below: A cavalry charge at the Battle of the Pelennor Fields, in front of Minus Tirith, where the armies of Gondor defeated the dark lord Sauron's forces.

sent forth a shaft that smote the face of the City. Then Pippin cried aloud, for the Tower of Ecthelion, standing high within the topmost wall, shone out against the sky, glimmering like a spike of pearl and silver, tall and fair and shapely, and its pinnacle glittered as if it were wrought of crystals; and white banners broke and fluttered from the battlements in the morning breeze, and high and far he heard a clear ringing as of silver trumpets.

Minas Tirith has seven levels shaped like giant rings, stacked on top of one another. Each ring is surrounded by walls 100 feet (30 m) tall. The city is set against the base of Mount Mindolluin, at the end of the White Mountains. With the mountains at its back, Minas Tirith can only be attacked from the front. The citadel at the summit, the seventh level, rises up so that it is 1,000 feet (305 m) high, overlooking the plains of Pelennor Fields beyond the base of the city. In the far distance, the fires of Mount Doom can be seen glowing in the land of Mordor.

Each ring of the city's seven levels has a great gate. To make it more difficult for invaders to reach the top, the gates connecting the levels are not placed in a straight line, but are scattered in different directions.

Minas Tirith holds a tremendous army that can ride out on horseback to defend the city. Lining the city walls are more than 100 trebuchets, a kind of gigantic catapult that can hurl boulders into invading armies. The walls are also lined with thousands of archers, ready to let loose their deadly arrows at any enemy foolish enough to attack the fortress.

In *The Return of the King*, Minas Tirith was attacked by the dark forces of Mordor. Many brave souls perished, but the battle was finally won by the people of Gondor and their many heroes. The city of Minas Tirith survived. It still stands guard over the lands of Middle-earth, as it has for thousands of years.

Above: Aragorn leads his army out of Minis Tirith. *Below:* A fell beast swoops down upon the battlefield in front of Minis Tirith.

RIVENDELL

Rivendell is a magical place created by fantasy author J.R.R. Tolkien. It is a hidden city of refuge, built by the elves of Middle-earth. Rivendell is in the foothills of the Misty Mountains, hidden away from the outside world by a deep, secret valley.

Rivendell blends in with the natural beauty of the mountains, with rivers, waterfalls, and woodlands surrounding the city. It is a legendary place, thousands of years old. Tolkein wrote that Rivendell was "The Last Homely House East of the Sea." It is a special place where elves live in harmony with nature.

In *The Hobbit*, the halfling Bilbo Baggins, along with a company of dwarves, visits Rivendell on his adventure to find a treasure stolen by the dragon Smaug.

In *The Lord of the Rings*, Frodo Baggins and his hobbit friends travel to Rivendell. They take part in a meeting of men, elves, and dwarves, who must decide what to do about the fate of the One Ring, the golden ring that contains the terrible power of the evil Sauron. The Lord of Rivendell, the 6,000-year-old elf named Elrond, presides over the meeting. It is there, in Rivendell, that they decide the One Ring must be destroyed within the fires of Mount Doom, and that little Frodo Baggins must carry the burden.

In the artificial language of Sindarin, which Tolkien created for his Middle-earth stories, the name for Rivendell is Imladris, which means "deep valley of the cleft."

Facing page: A view of Rivendell, used in the making of director Peter Jackson's epic *Lord of the Rings* films. *Below:* Frodo gazes at Rivendell in *Fellowship of the Ring.*

Xanadu

 anadu is the mysterious ancient city built by Kublai Khan, the Mongolian warrior-statesman who ruled China from 1260 to 1294. Kublai was the first emperor of the Yüan, or Mongol, Dynasty. He was the grandson of Genghis Khan. When he was given the throne and made Grand Khan, he turned away from his brutal, land-hungry ancestors and became a new kind of ruler. Kublai Khan tried to help his people. He gave them religious freedoms, created aid agencies, improved roads, and even established paper money.

The Mongol Empire covered most of Asia. Under Kublai Kahn's rule, the winter capitol was moved from Mongolian territory to Dadu, the site of modern-day Beijing, the capitol of China. In 1256, Kublai established what would become a separate summer palace in a place called Shangdu (also Shang-tu), which today many people call Xanadu.

Xanadu was known as the "city of 108 temples." Modern archaeological digs show that it had a square-shaped "Outer City," and a walled "Inner City" containing official buildings. There was a huge central palace made of marble where Kublai

Right: Marco Polo kneels in front of Kublai Kahn.

Above: The Forbidden City.

Khan stayed to escape the summer heat. The west and north walls enclosed a magnificent park with springs, sprawling lawns, and wandering animals.

In 1275, the Venetian explorer Marco Polo visited Xanadu. When he returned home, his tales of the marvelous city sparked a new interest in exploring the lands of the Far East.

Xanadu was sacked and burned during Chinese rebellions in 1358 and 1363. But the city will always be remembered as a magical, luxurious place.

In 1816, English poet Samuel Taylor Coleridge wrote a poem called *Kubla Khan*. It's a masterpiece of visionary enchantment, with descriptions of Xanadu that have echoed through the years:

> *In Xanadu did Kubla Khan*
> *A stately pleasure-dome decree:*
> *Where Alph, the sacred river, ran*
> *Through caverns measureless to man*
> *Down to a sunless sea.*
> *So twice five miles of fertile ground*
> *With walls and towers were girdled round:*
> *And there were gardens bright with sinuous rills,*
> *Where blossomed many an incense-bearing tree;*
> *And here were forests ancient as the hills,*
> *Enfolding sunny spots of greenery.*
> —Samuel Taylor Coleridge

Below: Kublai Kahn.

29

Glossary

ANGLO-SAXONS

The Germanic people who dominated England from the time of their arrival in the 5th century until the Norman Conquest of 1066. Today it also refers to anyone of English descent.

BARBARIAN

A term used in the Middle Ages for anyone who didn't belong to one of the "great" civilizations such as the Greeks or Romans, or from the Christian kingdoms such as France or Britain.

CHIVALRY

A code of conduct, a kind of way that a knight lived his life. Chivalry demanded bravery, courtesy, generosity, a willingness to help the weak, and most importantly, an undying loyalty to king and country.

FOLKLORE

The unwritten traditions, legends, and customs of a culture. Folklore is usually passed down by word of mouth from generation to generation.

INFANTRY

Soldiers who march or fight mostly on foot.

KNIGHTS OF THE ROUND TABLE

The legendary group of knights who swore loyalty to King Arthur and who lived at the castle of Camelot. The Round Table was a large table where many knights could sit together in a circle. In that way, no one knight was more important than another. In addition to King Arthur, some of the most famous knights who sat at the Round Table included Sir Lancelot, Sir Gawain, Sir Gareth, Sir Kay, Sir Bedevere, Sir Bors, Sir Bedevire, and Sir Galahad.

MEDIEVAL

Something from the Middle Ages.

MIDDLE AGES
In European history, a period defined by historians as roughly between 476 A.D. and 1450 A.D.

NORSE
The people, language, or culture of Scandinavia, especially medieval Scandinavia.

PROVINCE
A division or part of certain countries or empires. In ancient Roman history, lands controlled by the Romans, but located outside of Italy, were called provinces, and were run by provincial governors.

QUEST
A long, difficult search for something important. When the knights of Camelot were searching for the Holy Grail, they were said to be on a quest.

TAPESTRY
A kind of cloth decoration, many of which are brilliantly colored with fine patterns or scenes, that hang on castle walls. In addition to being pretty to look at, tapestries helped keep out cold drafts that often blew through castle walls.

TREBUCHET
A kind of catapult that looks like a giant sling, used mainly to hurl huge boulders at castles to break down the walls.

TSUNAMI
A large sea wave caused by an earthquake, volcanic eruption, landslide, or other undersea disturbance. Tsunamis can be incredibly destructive when they crash onto land. In December 2004, a tsunami caused by a huge earthquake killed hundreds of thousands of people in south Asia.

UTOPIA
An imaginary place where everybody and everything is perfect. The word was first used by author Sir Thomas More in his 1516 book *Utopia*. The opposite of a utopia is called a *dystopia*.

INDEX